WORLDS COLLIDE IN
EARLY AMERICA:
BEGINNINGS THROUGH 1620

by Gail Terp

Content Consultant
Edward M. Cook Jr.
Associate Professor of History
University of Chicago

CORE
LIBRARY

Published by ABDO Publishing Company, PO Box 398166, Minneapolis, MN 55439. Copyright © 2014 by Abdo Consulting Group, Inc. International copyrights reserved in all countries. No part of this book may be reproduced in any form without written permission from the publisher. The Core Library™ is a trademark and logo of ABDO Publishing Company.

Printed in the United States of America,
North Mankato, Minnesota
102013
012014
♻ THIS BOOK CONTAINS AT LEAST 10% RECYCLED MATERIALS.

Editor: Lauren Coss
Series Designer: Becky Daum

Library of Congress Control Number: 2013945900

Cataloging-in-Publication Data
Terp, Gail.
 Worlds collide in early America: beginnings through 1620 / Gail Terp.
    p. cm. -- (The story of the United States)
Includes bibliographical references and index.
ISBN 978-1-62403-171-7
1. America--Discovery and exploration--Juvenile literature.   2. United States--Social life and customs--To 1620--Juvenile literature. I. Title.
973.1--dc23
                                                              2013945900

Photo Credits: North Wind/North Wind Picture Archives, cover, 1, 6, 12, 15, 17, 21, 22, 28, 31, 34, 36, 45; Thinkstock, 4; National Geographic Society/Corbis, 9; Red Line Editorial, 10, 24; Heritage Images/Corbis, 18; Blue Lantern Studio/Corbis, 26; Photos.com/Thinkstock, 40

Cover: Jamestown colonists meet Native Americans in what is now Virginia.

CONTENTS

CHAPTER ONE

THE NATIVE-AMERICAN WORLD

People have lived in North America for thousands of years. Through the work of archaeologists, we are beginning to learn more about how and when they first came here.

Archaeologists don't know for sure how people first traveled to North America. Some people believe they crossed a narrow strip of land between Alaska and Russia. Others say they arrived by sea from

Ancient Native-American rock art can be found in locations across North America, including the Three Rivers Petroglyph Site in New Mexico.

Many Native Americans in the Northeast lived in longhouses with other members of their community.

Asia. Archaeologists also don't know when the first people got here. Most agree they came at least 12,000 to 14,000 years ago. No one knows how many people lived in North American before European explorers arrived during the late 1400s. Some scholars believe there were between 8 and 12 million Native Americans on the continent.

Archaeologists may not know for certain how or when the first people came to North America, but they do know the areas where they settled. Native Americans lived in all parts of the continent.

The Northeast

Two main groups of Native Americans lived in the Northeast. They were the Algonquian and the Iroquois. Both groups supported themselves with farming, hunting, and fishing. They also gathered plants, berries, and nuts.

Iroquois Lacrosse

The Iroquois played a game called lacrosse. Players used sticks with a cup or a net at one end. The cup was used to catch a ball made of soft deerskin. Players could not touch the ball with their hands. They scored points by hurling or carrying the ball past the other team's goal. The goals could be as far as three miles (4.8 km) apart. The game was fun, but it was likely also a way to train for battle. Today lacrosse is still a popular sport across North America.

Cahokia

The groups who lived in the Mississippi River Valley formed the Mississippian Culture. Most of these groups were later known as Mound Builders. They were called this because each village had several large mounds of earth. Native Americans often used these mounds as burial grounds where they buried their dead. Cahokia was an ancient Native-American trading center in what is now Illinois. Archaeologists believe it was built around the year 700 CE. Cahokia was one of the largest of the Mound Builders' towns.

The Southeast and the Plains

Native-American groups in the Southeast lived in two major regions. One was in the Mississippi River Valley. The other was along the Atlantic Coast. The people in both regions fed themselves by farming, hunting, fishing, and gathering.

The Plains is a mostly dry region in central North America. The Native Americans living on the Plains supported themselves with farming, hunting, and gathering. They hunted buffalo more than any other animal.

Buffalo hunts often lasted for weeks. Sometimes an entire village was part of a hunt.

The Southwest and the West

The Southwest was also home to several Native American groups, including the Pueblo, the Apache, the Navaho, and the Pima. Each group supported itself by farming, hunting, fishing, and gathering.

The Far West is the region that is now California and Nevada's Great Basin. Native Americans in this region lived in small villages. They supported

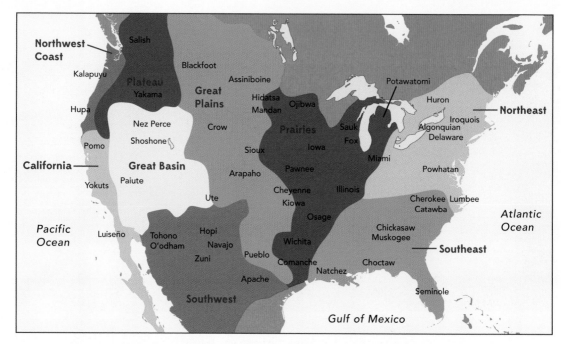

Native-American Regions in North America

This map shows where different Native-American groups lived across North America. Compare this map to the information you read in this chapter. Does seeing this map help you understand why Native Americans developed lifestyles that fit the land, food sources, and climates of the places they called home?

themselves by gathering nuts and seeds. They also hunted and fished. Some groups farmed.

The Native Americans who lived along the Northwest Coast had plentiful sources of food. They ate many kinds of fish. Sometimes they even went whale hunting. Native Americans in this region survived by hunting and gathering. They did not farm.

EXPLORE ONLINE

The focus of Chapter One is Native-American groups in North America. The Web site at the link below discusses the Plains Native Americans and buffalo hunting. As you know, every source is different. What new information can you learn from this Web site?

The Role of the Buffalo
www.mycorelibrary.com/worlds-collide-in-early-america

For thousands of years, Native-American life in North America continued with few major changes. Then, during the 1500s, European explorers began coming to North America in greater numbers. Life for the Native Americans would never be the same.

CHAPTER TWO

ACROSS THE ATLANTIC

The 1500s were a time of great change for the countries of Europe. Trade and exploration were expanding. Improvements in ships made travel to faraway lands possible. European ships were now able to sail to Africa and India. They were also able to sail to North and South America, which were often referred to as the New World.

European ships often carried explorers, who brought back new goods and stories of exciting lands.

Leif Eriksson and the Vikings

The Vikings were a group of seafaring warriors from the countries of Northern Europe, including Denmark, Sweden, and Norway. Leif Eriksson was a Viking from Greenland. He sailed west during the year 1000 CE. He stopped in what is now Newfoundland, Canada. He and his crew built a small settlement before sailing back to Greenland. Other Vikings returned to North America and lived in the settlement for several years before abandoning it completely.

Exploration

The first Scandinavian explorers reached North America in approximately 1000 CE. By the mid-1400s, other European nations were interested in the New World.

Europeans began exploring and trading beyond their lands for several reasons. During the 1500s, Asia produced many goods, including silk and spices. The trade routes between Europe and Asia were long and difficult. Traders could sail south and east around the tip of Africa, or they could travel east across the land. Some explorers thought they could find a shorter route by sailing west.

Native Americans traded furs, such as beaver pelts, with European explorers.

Explorers also hoped to discover riches such as gold and silver in the New World. Gold from Mexico and South America brought high profits for some explorers. Other explorers in North America sought different goods, such as fish and animal fur.

The goal of many explorations was to bring Christianity to the people of the New World. During the 1500s and 1600s, some of the countries of Europe were at war with each other. Most of the conflict was between people belonging to two main divisions of Christianity: Catholics and Protestants. The Catholic

Life in Europe

During the early 1500s, 80 to 90 percent of Europeans lived on farms. Most farmers did not own their land. They rented it from large landowners. These farms were in or near villages. The villages ranged in size. In larger towns and cities, many people were craftsmen.

countries included Spain, Portugal, and France. The Protestant countries included Great Britain and the Netherlands. Each division felt it knew Christianity best. As European nations began expanding their control across the globe, each country hoped to spread its own views of Christianity in the New World.

The Beginnings of the Slave Trade

Not all of the first travelers to the New World came from Europe. Beginning during the 1500s, European slave traders brought many West Africans across the Atlantic Ocean as slaves. These traders captured African people. The traders then shipped their captives to Portuguese and Spanish colonies in

Slave traders took Africans away from their homes and families and shipped them across the Atlantic Ocean to be sold as slaves.

South America and the Caribbean. There they were sold or traded as slaves.

Most slaves were forced by their owners to work in fields growing crops. They were not paid for their labor, and most would be enslaved for life. During the early 1600s, the slave trade expanded into the British colonies in North America.

CHAPTER THREE

EARLY EXPLORERS

Italian explorer Christopher Columbus set sail from Europe with three ships in 1492. He was hoping to find a route from Europe to Asia. The Spanish king and queen paid for his voyage. In October Columbus landed in the Bahamas and sailed throughout the Caribbean looking for riches. He took hundreds of Native Americans as slaves. But he never found the

Christopher Columbus's ships left Spain on August 3, 1492. He arrived in the Caribbean in October.

The Beginnings of Trade

Native Americans and Europeans had traded goods since the Vikings first came to North America. The first Europeans who came to North America after the Vikings were fishermen from Spain, France, and other countries in the late 1400s. The local people brought these fishermen furs to trade. The fishermen brought metal goods, such as knives, axes, pots, and pans. Native Americans traded these European goods with other Native Americans. Over the years, the goods and tales of the European traders made their way far into North America.

trade route to Asia or the riches he had been hoping for.

In 1497 explorer John Cabot sailed across the Atlantic to Canada for Great Britain. He was searching for a sea route to Asia known as the Northwest Passage. These early voyages were the beginning of an era of exploration for European nations.

Spain and Portugal funded many of these voyages. By the early 1500s, Spain had established settlements in South America and

Cabot did not find the Northwest Passage. But he claimed Canada for Britain's King Henry VII.

modern-day Mexico. These settlements were very profitable for Spain. Soon the country had built an empire that included much of South America and Mexico. In 1565 the Spanish built the settlement of Saint Augustine in what is now Florida. This was the first successful, permanent settlement in what would one day become the United States.

Giovanni da Verrazano

Spain and Portugal weren't the only countries hoping to make their mark in the New World. Other countries

Giovanni da Verrazano

hoped to recreate Spain's financial success there. In 1524 Italian explorer Giovanni da Verrazano sailed to North America. Verrazano sailed for the king of France. Like Columbus, he was looking for a new route to Asia. Verrazano arrived on the coast of what is now North Carolina. He then sailed north to New England and on to Canada.

Verrazano wrote about his travels. He described the lands he saw and the people he met. Many of his contacts with the Native Americans were positive. They welcomed him with food. They traded furs for his goods. At other times, Native Americans met Verrazano's ship with arrows and refused to let him anchor his boat.

Exploring the South

Alvar Nuñez Cabeza de Vaca was a Spanish explorer. He was one of the first explorers to make his way into western North America. In 1528 he was part of a group heading to Mexico to

Fur Mania

Furs were some of the most commonly traded goods between Native Americans and Europeans in what is now the northern United States and Canada. At first small furs such as marten and fox were most popular. Then, during the late 1500s, beaver hats became popular in Europe. The demand for beaver fur soared. But when Europe developed beaver mania, beavers became extinct in parts of North America. This was because hunters killed so many of the animals.

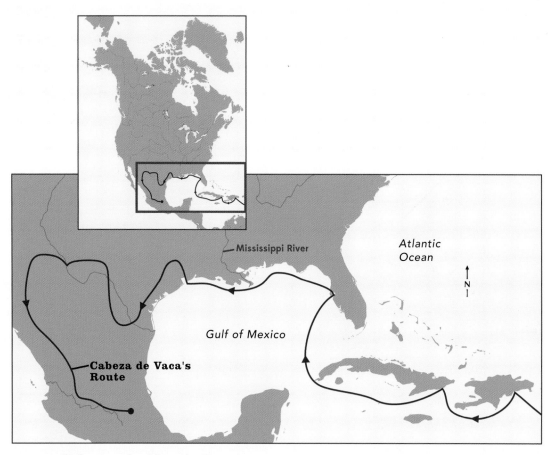

Cabeza de Vaca's Route

This map shows the route some historians believe Cabeza de Vaca may have taken during his eight-year journey in North America. What challenges might he have faced on his travels? Compare this map to the map in Chapter One. What Native-American groups might Cabeza de Vaca have encountered?

start a settlement. A storm at sea caused a shipwreck.

Cabeza de Vaca was separated from his group.

For years Cabeza de Vaca explored what

are now the southern states, traveling through

Native-American land. Sometimes he was captured by local tribes and enslaved. Other times he traveled freely and was treated well by Native-American groups. He covered thousands of miles, traveling along the Gulf of Mexico coast through Florida and west as far as Texas. Eventually he traveled south into Mexico. Eight years after he started, a group from Spain found him. Cabeza de Vaca sailed home to Spain with them.

Hernando de Soto

Starting in 1539, Hernando de Soto also explored what are now the southern states. He was also from Spain. His goal was to find gold and set up a colony in North America. He began in Florida and traveled north to North Carolina. He turned southwest and traveled as far as Texas. Along the way, he gathered a great fortune. He did this by stealing whatever he wanted. He kidnapped Native Americans and chained them together as slaves.

De Soto was likely the first European to cross the Mississippi River.

De Soto and his men spread disease as they traveled. By capturing Native Americans to be used as slaves, he exposed them to European germs. The people he captured had no immunity to these new germs. Many died while they were captives. The ones who escaped brought the germs back to their villages. The diseases spread by de Soto and other explorers wiped out entire Native-American villages.

When Giovanni da Verrazano made his trip up the North American coast, one of his sailors swam to shore. As he was swimming back to the ship, a wave swept the sailor back toward shore. In a letter to the king, Verrazano described how the Native Americans on shore responded:

> *Seeing this, the native people immediately ran up; they took [the sailor] by the head, the legs, and arms and carried him some distance away. . . . They took off his shirt and shoes and hose, leaving him naked, then made a huge fire next to him, placing him near the heat. . . . After remaining with them for a while, he regained his strength, and showed them by signs that he wanted to return to the ship. With the greatest kindness, they accompanied him to the sea, holding him close and embracing him; and then to reassure him, they withdrew to a high hill and stood watching him until he was in the boat.*
>
> *Source: Giovanni da Verrazano. "Letter to King Francis I of France." July 8, 1524. National Humanities Center. National Humanities Center, n.d. Web. Accessed August 19, 2013.*

What's the Big Idea?

What does this passage tell you about what Verrazano thought of the Native Americans? How does it seem the Native Americans felt about the sailor?

CHAPTER FOUR

FURTHER EXPLORATION

European nations continued exploring North America throughout the 1500s. But only Spain had established permanent colonies on the continent. During the 1580s, Great Britain was at war with Spain. The British wanted a colony in North America to give it a base from which to fight. From there it could battle Spanish ships along the Atlantic Coast.

In the 1580s, Great Britain's conflict with Spain played a part in encouraging the British to establish a colony in North America.

Great Britain also hoped to profit from increased trade with the local Native Americans.

Roanoke Colony

In 1584 two British ships landed off the coast of what is now North Carolina. The captains and crew explored the area and found woods filled with deer and rabbits. One island, which they called Roanoke, looked like a good spot for a settlement. The British returned home to report their findings.

The following year, five large ships and two smaller ones returned. The ships carried British settlers hoping to build a colony on Roanoke Island. The colonists sent messages asking to meet the local people. They were the Secotan people, who were Algonquian. The two sides did not trust one another. This led to conflicts. However, in the end, the Secotan granted permission for the settlers to build a settlement on Roanoke Island.

Over the next several months, the relationship between the settlers and the local people grew

Roanoke colonists built their settlement on an island off the coast of North Carolina.

difficult. Epidemics caused by the germs brought by the settlers swept through the region. Many Secotan people died. The Secotan chief had been giving the settlers food. He stopped this after the epidemic hit his people. The settlers had not grown crops, so they had little to eat. In 1587 Roanoke governor John White returned to Great Britain for more supplies.

Henry Hudson

Henry Hudson was a British explorer determined to find a route to Asia. In 1607 and 1608, he sailed two voyages for a British company. He tried to reach Asia by sailing north, over the North Pole. Then he tried to sail north of Russia. Both attempts failed. In 1609 Hudson made another attempt for a Dutch company. He sailed up the Hudson River. On his way, he traded with the local people and explored the islands in the harbor. Then he continued upriver. Hudson never found a route to Asia. But he reported what he had seen when he returned to Europe. This sparked an interest in more travel to the area.

It took White three years to get a ship to bring him back to North America. When he returned to Roanoke in 1590, he found no people at the settlement. Historians still don't know what happened to the Roanoke Colony and its settlers.

Samuel de Champlain

The French were also hoping to build a colony in the New World. Samuel de Champlain was an explorer from France. He was also a mapmaker who was known for his accuracy and detail. He kept careful journals of his travels. From

1604 to 1606, Champlain made three voyages along the coast of New England. The goal of all three trips was to find sites for French settlements in New England. The first voyage explored the coast of what is now Maine. The second and third voyages went as far as Cape Cod in Massachusetts.

On his first trip, Champlain was the captain. He made positive contacts with the local people he met. He approached them with just a few men. They kept their weapons out

Champlain's Alliance

As a sign of friendship, the Montagnais, Huron, and Algonquian asked Champlain to join them in a war against the Iroquois. In 1609 Champlain and his allies traveled to Iroquois land near what is now Lake Champlain. The battle that followed was a short one. Champlain and two of his men fired their guns. Three Iroquois chiefs were killed. The Iroquois quickly fled. However, this short battle caused the Iroquois and the French to remain enemies for years to come. More than 100 years later, the Iroquois helped the British defeat the French in the French and Indian War (1754–1763).

Champlain allied with the Algonquian, Huron, and Montagnais to fight the Iroquois near Lake Champlain, which was later named for the explorer.

of sight. He treated the people he met with respect. Champlain became allies with three tribes, the Montagnais, the Huron, and the Algonquian.

However, on his second and third trips, Champlain was not the captain. The captains on these trips dealt poorly with the Native Americans. Sometimes they marched among the local people with guns showing. They took food without permission. This destroyed the good relationships Champlain had built.

CHAPTER FIVE

CHANGES IN BOTH WORLDS

Great Britain didn't give up on colonizing the New World after the failure of Roanoke. In April 1607 British ships arrived in what is now Virginia. They spent two weeks scouting. They also met the local people, the Powhatan, who were Algonquian. Both groups were on guard. The British wanted to build a colony. The Powhatan did not want to give up their land.

After the settling of Jamestown Colony, European and Native-American interaction would be more frequent than ever before.

Thomas Savage

Both the British and the Native Americans wanted to understand one another's languages. To help with this, they sometimes traded men to act as interpreters. In 1608 the colonists traded 13-year-old Thomas Savage to the Powhatan. His job was to live with the Powhatan people and learn their culture and language. The Powhatan treated Thomas well. He lived with them for three years. After that, he continued his job as interpreter.

The Jamestown Colony

During the next few months, the settlers built a fort at the Jamestown site. For the next several years, the colonists and the Powhatan worked to maintain good relations. However, frequent conflicts about resources and who had the right to the land occurred between the two groups. Sometimes these conflicts resulted in violence. But the Jamestown Colony survived.

A Changing Continent

The Jamestown Colony was the first of many successful British colonies in North America.

Soon more British colonists were settling what is now the United States. The Europeans who came to the New World encountered new land and people. They also encountered new foods. In their new homes, settlers planted many of the crops the local people grew. These crops included maize (corn), potatoes, tomatoes, and peanuts.

Some Europeans brought these foods back to their countries to cultivate. The new foods enriched Europeans' diets.

Colonists also brought many new plants to the New World. They brought wheat, fruit trees, grapevines, sugarcane, melons, and more. The new crops did well in the right conditions.

Slavery in Jamestown

In 1619 a Dutch ship sailed into Virginia. It had just captured approximately 20 African slaves from a ship off the coast of Mexico. The Dutch ship needed supplies, so the captain traded the slaves to the Jamestown settlers for food. The slaves were most likely put to work in the local tobacco fields. These were the first African slaves in a British colony in America.

Horses were especially helpful to the Plains people. They used them to hunt buffalo.

The Europeans brought livestock to the New World. Before European explorers arrived, Native Americans had never seen horses, cattle, chickens, sheep, or goats. The new animals eventually spread across the continent.

Native-American and European cultures had much to share. As more Europeans arrived in North America, both Native-American and European cultures would be changed permanently. Life would never be the same.

Chief Powhatan led the Powhatan people. In 1609 he met with Jamestown leader John Smith. Smith wrote down Chief Powhatan's words:

> *Why should you take by force that from us which you can have by love? Why should you destroy us, who have provided you with food? What can you get by war? . . . What is the cause of your jealousy? You see us unarmed, and willing to supply your wants, if you will come in a friendly manner, and not with swords and guns, as to invade an enemy . . .*
>
> *I, therefore, exhort you to peaceable councils; and, above all, I insist that the guns and swords, the cause of all our jealousy and uneasiness, be removed and sent away.*
>
> Source: Native American Testimony: A Chronicle of Indian-White Relations from Prophecy to the Present, 1492–1992. *Ed. Peter Nabokov. New York: Penguin, 1991. Print. 72–73.*

Consider Your Audience

When John Smith returned to the Jamestown settlement, he might have tried to tell the other settlers about what Chief Powhatan had said. Imagine you are trying to convey Chief Powhatan's words to a modern audience, such as your friends or family. Write a blog post conveying this information to the new audience.

1000

1492

1497

Viking Leif Eriksson sails to Newfoundland in Canada looking for a place to settle.

Italian explorer Christopher Columbus sails to North America while searching for a trade route to Asia.

Explorer John Cabot sails to Canada, which he claims for Great Britain's King Henry VII.

1584

1604

1607

The first ships arrive at what becomes Great Britain's Roanoke Island settlement.

Samuel de Champlain begins his three voyages along the coast of what is now New England.

The first ships arrive at what becomes the Jamestown settlement.

1524

Giovanni da Verrazano sails to North America looking for a new route to Asia.

1528

Alvar Nuñez Cabeza de Vaca starts his eight-year exploration of what is now the southern United States.

1539

Hernando de Soto begins his explorations of the southern United States.

1608

Thirteen-year-old Thomas Savage begins living with the Powhatan people to learn their culture and language.

1609

Henry Hudson sails up the Hudson River looking for a shorter route to Asia.

1619

The first African slaves in a British colony are brought to America.

Why Do I Care?

It has been more than 400 years since Europeans began exploring North America. But events that happened so long ago still affect your life. Chapter Five talks about foods Native Americans and Europeans introduced to one another. How might your life be different if these two groups hadn't shared resources and knowledge? Are there any foods you would miss if the Native Americans and the Europeans hadn't shared?

Tell the Tale

You read about a sailor from Giovanni da Verrazano's ship in Chapter Three. When the sailor got back to the ship safely, he must have told his shipmates about his adventure. Write the sailor's story as he might have told it to his shipmates. Use details from the chapter. Make sure to set the scene, develop a sequence of events, and include a conclusion.

Say What?

Studying long-ago times can mean learning new vocabulary. Find five words in this book that you didn't know. Look up the words in a dictionary. Then write the meanings in your own words, and use each word in a sentence.

Surprise Me

Chapters One and Two discuss what life was like in North America and Europe hundreds of years ago. After reading these chapters, what two or three things about life back then did you find most surprising? Write a few sentences about each fact. Why did you find it surprising?

GLOSSARY

allies
people, groups, or countries that have joined together for a particular purpose

archaeologist
a scientist who studies the past by examining historical sites and artifacts

captive
prisoner

craftsmen
people who specialize in producing a specific type of good

cultivate
to plant and help grow

epidemic
an outbreak of disease that spreads rapidly to many people

immunity
the condition of being able to resist a disease

interpreter
a person who helps people who speak different languages understand one another

Northwest Passage
the nonexistent sea route from Europe to Asia that many European explorers searched for

LEARN MORE

Books

Fritz, Jean, and Hudson Talbott. *The Lost Colony of Roanoke*. New York: G. P. Putnam's Sons, 2004.

Higgins, Melissa. *The Jamestown Colony*. Minneapolis: ABDO, 2013.

Huey, Lois Miner. *American Archaeology Uncovers the Earliest English Colonies*. New York: Marshall Cavendish, 2010.

Web Links

To learn more about early America, visit ABDO Publishing Company online at **www.abdopublishing.com**. Web sites about early America are featured on our Book Links page. These links are routinely monitored and updated to provide the most current information available.

Visit **www.mycorelibrary.com** for free additional tools for teachers and students.

INDEX

ABOUT THE AUTHOR

Gail Terp is a retired elementary teacher who has slipped into writing for kids and beginning readers. Her blog, *Best Blog for Kids Who Hate to Read*, is a family blog for reluctant readers and their families. Gail lives in Troy, New York.